- HOME SWEET HOME -

Sarah Tomczak is the author of four books, including the successful *How to Live Like a Lady*. She has been a journalist for over twelve years; her career includes stints in New York and London and she has written for everyone from *Us Weekly* to *Cosmopolitan, Glamour* to *Conde Nast Brides*. She currently lives in London.

To buy books in quantity for corporate use
or incentives, call **(800) 962–0973**
or e-mail **premiums@GlobePequot.com.**

Design and illustrations by Sarah Fotheringham
Additional text by Kelly Thompson

Library of Congress Cataloging-in-Publication Data is available on file.

ISBN 978-0-7627-8128-7

Printed in China

10 9 8 7 6 5 4 3 2 1

- HOME SWEET HOME -

REDISCOVERING THE JOYS OF DOMESTICITY WITH CLASSIC HOUSEHOLD PROJECTS AND RECIPES

Sarah Tomczak

LYONS PRESS
Guilford, Connecticut
An imprint of Globe Pequot Press

— Contents —

- INTRODUCTION -

In our modern age of rampant consumerism, many of us are losing touch with the traditional domestic activities that previous generations took for granted. We buy everything we need—and much that we don't—rather than making new or making do.

Especially in the kitchen, fewer people are taking the time to make or grow things themselves. But however convenient they might be, commercially-made products can never compare to the flavors and scents that you can create at home, or to the sense of accomplishment of rolling up your sleeves and making something from scratch. Mass-produced objects can never compete with the charm of items made with the love and care of your own hands, that are an expression of your individuality.

A generation or two ago, women knew how to keep an orderly and cost-effective home. Somehow they found time to raise children, keep an immaculate house, grow vegetables, make jam, do a spot of dressmaking, polish the silver, and bake bread, all without the aid of a fridge-freezer or microwave. Over the last fifty years new gadgets, technology, and ingredients have become increasingly available to us and dramatically changed our home lives. Yet the increasing number of domestic appliances in the home has not actually given us any more spare time—in fact, we seem to have less today than ever before—and in many ways have removed a sense of personal touch from our homes.

In these pages you will find 100 simple, traditional projects and pieces of advice that will help you to rediscover the enjoyment to be had in your own home, whether baking, crafting, cooking, cleaning, or decorating. Taking a renewed interest, and indeed a measure of pride, in your home and making it beautiful does not mean a blind return to old-fashioned values—you should see it as a rediscovery of the domestic skills that can introduce pleasure, creativity, and a strong sense of satisfaction into our lives. It is a chance to pick up some of the best forgotten talents of generations past—with a few modern twists to match our twenty-first-century lifestyles.

Dip in and discover how to: bake scones; make strawberry jam; keep your knives sharp; dry and preserve fruits and herbs; remove a variety of different tough stains; restore wood furniture; mix a classic martini; press flowers; make your own bubble bath; and plenty of other ways to experience the pleasure of creating from scratch and make the most of your time spent at home.

I hope that you will find this an invaluable sourcebook of traditional projects that will bring a unique charm into your life and your home.

- Traditional Strawberry Jam -

12 cups (1.5 kg) strawberries
Juice of one lemon
5½ cups (1.25 kg) sugar

Makes approximately 6 jars

Prepare the strawberries by removing all tops and greenery, and chopping the large fruits into smaller chunks.

Put the strawberries and the lemon juice into a saucepan and simmer very gently for an hour.

Add the sugar and turn up the heat until the mixture sets—
at around 220°F (105°C), if you have a cooking thermometer.

Skim any scum off the top, then set aside until a skin starts to form.

Pour into sterilized jars, seal them and let cool. Then label them and store in a cool place.

- BAKING BREAD -

3⅓ CUPS (500 G) GRANARY, WHOLEWHEAT, OR
WHITE BREAD FLOUR
¼ OZ (7 G) SACHET FAST-ACTION DRIED YEAST
1 TEASPOON SALT
1¼ CUP (300 ML) HAND-HOT WATER
2 TABLESPOONS OLIVE OIL
1 TABLESPOON CLEAR HONEY

Mix the flour, yeast, and salt together in a large bowl with your hands.

Mix the hot water with the oil and honey, then stir into the dry ingredients.

Place the dough on a lightly floured surface and knead until it no longer feels
sticky, sprinkling with a little more flour if needed.

Shape the dough as desired and place in a loaf tin, leaving room for
expansion. Put the tin in a large plastic food bag and leave to rise for another
hour, or until the dough no longer springs back when pressed.

Pre-heat the oven to 400°F (200°C). Make several slashes across the top of the
loaf with a sharp knife, then bake for approximately 30 minutes, or until the loaf
is risen and golden.

Remove from tin and place on a cooling rack, tapping the base to check if it is
cooked: It should sound hollow. Leave to cool before slicing and serving.

- GROWING TOMATOES -

If you're starting from seeds, fill a 3-inch (7.5-cm) pot with potting soil and lightly water. Scatter with a generous sprinkling of seeds and then add a thin layer of vermiculite—this is a natural mineral that insulates your seeds and helps them to grow; it is available at all good garden stores.

Place on a sunny windowsill to germinate—you should see your first seedlings in two weeks, and the plants should be strong enough to move into their own pots at eight weeks.

To transplant, hold each plant by its stem and leaves, gently digging into the soil to lift it out. Place each plant into its own 3-inch (7.5-cm) pot and water lightly. Once you can see roots coming through the drainage holes at the bottom, transplant into a 5-inch (12-cm) pot.

When the first branch of flowers appears, the tomato plants are ready to go into a larger pot, or growing bags. Break up the soil well before adding the plants, and scoop out enough soil to make room for the roots, ensuring that the ball of roots is fully covered by a layer of soil. Place a growing cane next to each plant, and as your plants grow, tie them to the cane at every 4 inches (10 cm).

To ensure you get the best tomatoes, once your plant has produced four flowering branches, snap out the growing stem from the top—and any shoots that grow in the leaf joints. You want one long, tall plant, as opposed to a bush, and this way the plant's energy will go into producing fruit.

Water your tomato plants every day, use fertilizer once a week, and keep in a sunny spot that's protected from the wind, ideally a greenhouse.

- MAKING A LAVENDER BAG -

Fragrantly scented sachets are a wonderful way to keep your wardrobes and drawers smelling fresh. They also make a lovely homemade gift.

Cut a rectangle from a piece of pretty fabric—about the size of a postcard.

Sew a $1/2$-inch (1-cm) hem along one long edge of the rectangle. This will be the top of your lavender bag, so make sure any pattern in the fabric is oriented the right way.

Fold the rectangle in half, the right side of the fabric facing inward, so that the two short edges come together.

Starting from just beneath the hem, sew a $1/4$-inch ($1/2$-cm) seam—to join the two short edges of the fabric. You should now have a fabric tube with the hemmed edge at the top.

Next, sew a $1/4$-inch ($1/2$-cm) seam along the bottom edge of the tube, to complete the bag.

Turn the fabric right side out, push out the corners fully, and press.

Thread a length of narrow ribbon through the hem at the top of the bag to make a drawstring. You can tie the ribbon to a safety pin to guide it through.

Fill the bag with a spoonful or two of dried lavender and pull the drawstring to close. Tie a double knot to keep it secure, and a bow to make it pretty.

Replace the lavender once every month or so.

- USING AROMATHERAPY -

Essential oils are a wonderful way to bring the healing benefits of aromatherapy into your life. They can be added to a hot bath, used to make pot pourri, burned in oil burners, or used as a massage oil.

LAVENDER
Good for insomnia and to calm and soothe, add 4 to 8 drops to your bath, or put 2 drops on your pillow.

MAY CHANG
Good for increasing energy levels, lifting your mood, and beating depression, put 5 to 6 drops in an oil burner, or 2 drops of may chang and frankincense oil in your bath for an energizing soak.

ROSEMARY
Used to stimulate and invigorate, mix 10 drops with a base carrier oil and rub on your hands and feet to help you think clearly.

- BLENDING A MASSAGE OIL -

To make a massage blend, first decide which scents soothe or invigorate you—do you prefer light and floral, zesty and fruity, or more woody and spicy fragrances?

Once you have made your choice, combine the essential oil(s) with a carrier oil such as sweet almond, grapeseed, or rosehip oil. Mix the carrier and essential oils together as per the ratio recommended on the bottle—this will vary from oil to oil. If storing your massage blend for future use, do so in a dark glass bottle away from direct heat or sunlight.

- Favorite Chocolate Brownies -

2¼ CUPS (200 G) DARK CHOCOLATE
½ CUP (100 G) UNSALTED BUTTER, SOFTENED
1⅓ CUPS (250 G) GRANULATED SUGAR
4 LARGE EGGS, BEATEN
1 TEASPOON VANILLA EXTRACT
⅔ CUP (60 G) ALL-PURPOSE FLOUR
⅔ CUP (60 G) COCOA POWDER

Makes 16 brownies

Preheat the oven to 350°F (180°C), grease a 8-inch (20-cm) baking pan, and line it with wax paper.

Break the dark chocolate into pieces and place in a bowl. Heat in a microwave on medium for 10 to 15 seconds, then check consistency. Repeat until the chocolate is smooth and fully melted. Set aside to cool slightly.

Put the butter and sugar into a bowl and beat with an electric mixer until light and fluffy, then gradually add the beaten eggs, mixing well after each.

Beat in vanilla extract, then pour in the cooled, melted chocolate and mix thoroughly. Sift the flour and cocoa powder into the mixture and gently fold in using a metal spoon. When fully combined, spoon the mixture into the prepared pan and spread evenly.

Bake in the oven for about 20 to 25 minutes until firm to the touch. It should be soft in the middle, but the top should be cracked. Let cool for at least 20 minutes in the pan. Then remove the brownie, place it on a cutting board, and cut into 2-inch (5-cm) squares.

- PAINTING A ROOM -

Take plenty of time choosing the right colors and finishes from the vast array of paints available these days: collect color cards, read the manufacturers' blurbs, and ask advice from in-store experts.

Once the decision has been made, don your old clothes and clear the room in question or move all furniture into the center. Cover all flooring and remaining furniture with dustsheets.

Prepare all surfaces by filling gaps, lightly sandpapering lumps, bumps, and woodwork, and wiping away any dust.

Paint the ceiling first, working across in parallel bands, wiping away any wall splashes immediately. Two coats are normally required.

Next apply an undercoat to the woodwork if required; bare wood will need a primer before the undercoat.

Once this is dry, start on the walls. Use a small brush to "cut in" around the edges of the woodwork and ceiling. If desired, you can use specialist masking tape for a straight finish on all edges. Then paint the main areas with a larger brush or roller, working from top to bottom. Complete each wall before moving on to the next. Always allow each coat to fully dry before applying the next; at least two coats are usually required.

Finally, apply the top coat to the woodwork.

If you need to leave your paint tray or brushes for an hour or two, wrap them tightly in saran wrap so they don't dry out. Be sure to thoroughly wash out brushes at the end of each job.

- Tangy Lemonade -

1¼ CUPS (240 G) SUGAR (ACCORDING TO TASTE)
1 CUP (250 ML) HOT WATER
1 CUP (250 ML) FRESHLY SQUEEZED LEMON JUICE
(ABOUT 4–6 LEMONS)
4 CUPS (1 LITER) COLD WATER
ICE CUBES
FRESH LEMON SLICES

Serves approximately 6

Dissolve the sugar in the hot water by heating it in a small saucepan over a low
heat. The resulting mixture is known as sugar syrup.

Add the lemon juice and the sugar syrup to a jug.

Add the cold water until the mixture reaches the desired strength.
Simply taste to try.

Put in the refrigerator for 30 to 40 minutes.

Serve with ice and a slice of lemon.

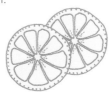

- Zesty Lemon Curd -

---

1 CUP (225 G) BUTTER
2 CUPS (450 G) SUGAR
3 TABLESPOONS LEMON ZEST
$^2/_3$ CUP (150 ML) LEMON JUICE
A PINCH OF SALT
4 EGGS

Makes approximately 1 liter (4 cups)

Melt the butter in a heatproof bowl over a pan of simmering water.

Pour in the sugar, the lemon zest and juice, and the salt.

Stir until the sugar has dissolved.

In a separate bowl, beat the eggs until frothy and stir in a good spoonful of the lemon mixture.

Return the mixture to the bowl over the simmering water and cook for 7 to 10 minutes, until thick.

Ladle into sterilized jars, cover and let cool.

Store in the refrigerator.

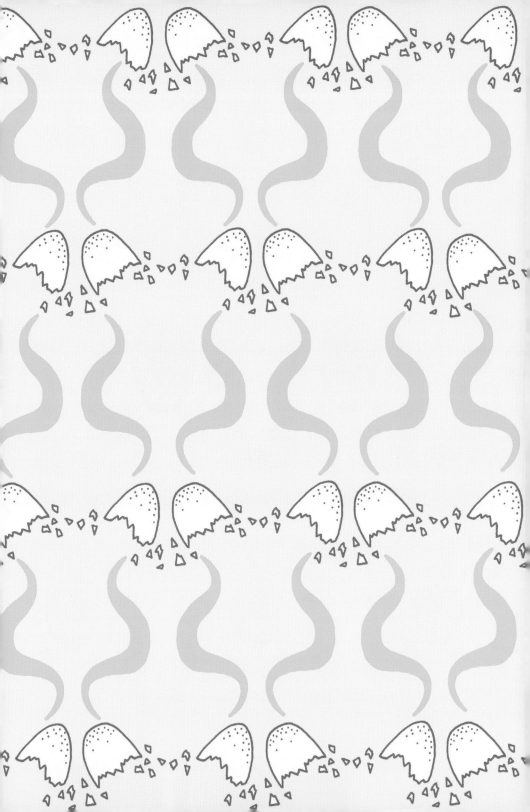

- DECENT CHOCOLATE TRUFFLES -

1¼ CUPS (280 G) DARK CHOCOLATE—IDEALLY 70% COCOA
1¼ CUPS (284 ML) HEAVY CREAM
¼ CUP (50 G) UNSALTED BUTTER
A PINCH OF SEA SALT

Makes approximately 50 truffles

Chop the chocolate into small pieces and place in a large bowl.

Put the cream and butter into a saucepan and heat gently, so that the butter
melts and the cream simmers.

Remove the saucepan from the heat and pour over the chocolate pieces. Stir,
so that the chocolate melts and you get a glossy smooth mixture. Add salt.

If you want to flavor your truffles, add your preferred flavoring now: Try
2 tablespoons of brandy, Grand Marnier, or coconut rum; the juice and zest of
an orange; a tablespoon of crystallized ginger; or a teaspoon of fresh chili.

Leave the mixture to cool, then chill in the refrigerator for at least 2 hours.

To shape your truffles into balls, dip a dessert spoon or melon baller into a cup of
boiling water and it will easily glide through your chocolate mixture.

To decorate your truffles, roll in toasted dried coconut or flaked almonds, or
sprinkle with cocoa powder or crystallized ginger. To coat in chocolate, melt
pieces of chocolate in a bowl over a saucepan of boiling water. Allow to cool
slightly, then spoon over the top until well-coated. Leave to cool and harden.

The truffles will keep in an airtight container for three days, or freeze for a month.

- Preparing a Picnic Basket -

Use an old-fashioned wicker basket if you can—for a traditional feel. Then simply fill it (possibly using a second bag to lessen the weight of each one) with all the essentials for the required number of people.

꙳   Eating utensils, including plates, cutlery, napkins, cups and/or glasses, a corkscrew for wine if desired.

꙳   A range of drinks, such as water, juice, sodas, and possibly a bottle of wine, if appropriate. You may want to include hot drinks as well, in which case, pack a flask of hot water, some milk, sugar, and tea or coffee.

꙳   Sandwiches are a picnic staple. Try egg, tuna, cheese and pickle, or ham and cheese. Avoid ingredients that will make the bread soggy, or pack them in a separate container so that you can add them in just before you eat.

꙳   A choice of dips with crudités and/or potato chips.

꙳   A selection of fruit, such as strawberries, grapes, and raspberries.

꙳   Some sweet treats such as cookies or brownies.

꙳   Take along a few ice packs for the food and drinks that will need them. You may want to take a separate cooler to keep these items in.

꙳   You'll also need a cozy blanket or two to sit on—plus a couple of quaint tablecloths to place over them so that they don't get dirty.

꙳   Remember to bring a couple of trash bags for clearing up.

- PEPPERMINT TEA -

Both caffeine- and calorie-free, peppermint tea is known to aid digestion, which makes it particularly soothing to drink after a meal, and you can make yourself a cup simply from leaves grown in your own garden.

Boil the desired amount of water, depending on how many cups you want to make.

Place the mint in a teapot: Allow 1 heaping teaspoon per cup for dried leaves or a couple of sprigs per cup for fresh, depending on how strong you like it.

Pour the water over the leaves and allow to steep for 5 to 10 minutes.

Pour through a strainer into a cup and add sugar or honey to taste if desired.

- TIMESAVING TIPS -

❧ Keep a set of cleaning tools in a cupboard on each floor of your house so you don't waste time running up and down the stairs.

❧ An adhesive roller for removing lint is useful for all sorts of surfaces, particularly for removing stray pet hairs from clothes, chairs, or rugs.

❧ Pour some bleach into the lavatory once or twice a week—a good soaking prevents deposits from building up.

❧ A little furniture polish sprayed onto skirting boards and door frames acts as a dust repellent.

❧ Line waste bins with plastic carrier bags—not just a way of putting plastic bags to good use, it makes emptying the bins a much easier job.

- Perfect Scones -

---

1 CUP (225 G) SELF-RISING FLOUR
A PINCH OF SALT
$\frac{1}{3}$ CUP (75 G) BUTTER, AT ROOM TEMPERATURE
3 TABLESPOONS GOLDEN SUPERFINE SUGAR
ONE LARGE EGG
2 TABLESPOONS BUTTERMILK, PLUS EXTRA FOR GLAZING
$\frac{1}{4}$ CUP (50 G) RAISINS (OPTIONAL)

Makes approximately 10 scones

Heat your oven to 425°F (220°C).

Sift the flour and salt into a large mixing bowl, cut the butter into small pieces, and rub this into the flour mixture with your fingertips until it looks like breadcrumbs. Then mix in the superfine sugar.

Beat together the egg and buttermilk, then add to the flour mixture in four parts, along with the raisins, if using, stirring with a spatula as it binds together, to form a dough.

When the mixture has become a ball, lift it out of the bowl and onto a floured surface. Using a rolling pin, lightly roll out the dough until it's 1 inch (2.5 cm) thick.

Using a 2-inch (5-cm) round cutter, cut out as many scones as possible (it should make about a dozen), gathering the scraps together to roll out again.

Place the scones on a greased baking tray and brush with a bit more buttermilk, then bake for 10 to 12 minutes until your scones have risen and are golden brown.

Serve warm with salted butter or cool with clotted cream and jam.

- REPAIRING A HEM -

PINS
NEEDLE
THREAD (A CLOSE MATCH TO THE ORIGINAL)

Begin by turning the garment inside out. From the "inside" of the fabric, lightly press the ripped section to its original position. This will help to hold the fabric in place as you work.

Carefully pin the loose part of the hem in place. Pins are best placed parallel to the bottom edge, half way between the top and bottom of the hem, so you don't have to remove them while you sew.

Start and finish your repair an inch or two on either side of the ripped section (i.e., within the secure section), so that your first stitches reinforce the existing stitching.

Secure your stitching at both the start and end of your repair with a few small stitches repeated on top of one another (backstitches). Make these securing stitches in the turned up section of the hem, not the front part of the garment, so that they aren't visible during wear.

Copy the existing stitch pattern of the garment as closely as possible. Stitches should be about half an inch (1 cm) apart—do not pull the thread taut.

To make your hemming as inconspicuous as possible, use the tiniest stitches you can. Pick up just one or two fibers of the fabric with each stitch, taking alternately one from the hem, then one from the garment, until the repair is complete.

- COOKING THE PERFECT ROAST -

When it comes to a roast the timing is the most important thing. The easiest way to get it right is to decide on a time to serve dinner and then work backward. Give yourself 10 minutes extra breathing time when working it all out—no matter how organized you are, things will take a bit longer than you anticipate.

Work out how long your joint needs to cook—the general rule is 20 minutes per pound of meat and then 20 minutes extra, although of course it depends on the type of meat and the temperature. Ask your butcher's advice if you are unsure.

To eat at 2:00 PM, work the cooking time backward from 1:30 PM to find out when the meat needs to go into the oven. Don't forget to take the meat out of the refrigerator well in advance to get it to room temperature before you start.

Roast potatoes will take the next longest time to cook. Par-boil them first for a superior finish. They should be crunchy and chewy on the outside, but soft and fluffy on the inside.

Apply the same principle to the vegetables and any other accompaniments you are serving, like stuffing: Calculate how long they take to cook and work backward from 2:00 PM to know when to put them in the oven.

The gravy should be the last thing you do: When you have removed the meat from the roasting tray to rest, pour the meat juices from the tray into a saucepan, scraping down the sides and base of the pan. Add wine, stock, or both to the pan, and leave to boil until reduced to the desired consistency.

- EASY GUACAMOLE DIP -

---

1 LARGE TOMATO
3 VERY RIPE AVOCADOS
1 SMALL RED ONION, FINELY CHOPPED
1 SMALL RED CHILI, DESEEDED AND FINELY CHOPPED
THE JUICE OF ONE LARGE LIME
A BUNCH OF CILANTRO, CHOPPED
SEA SALT AND FRESHLY GROUND BLACK PEPPER

Serves 4

Finely chop the tomato and scrape into a large bowl, including the pulp and all the juice.

Halve and pit the avocados, chop roughly, and add to the bowl, along with the onion, chili, lime juice, and chopped cilantro (leaves and stalks).

Mash all the ingredients together roughly and season with salt and pepper.

To stop your guacamole from going brown, sit one of the avocado pits on top of the guacamole or cover with saran wrap and press this down onto the mixture to stop too much air getting to it (the lime juice should help prevent this as well).

- Celery Salt -

The leaves from one bunch of celery
Sea salt

Pick the leaves from each celery stalk, then rinse in cold water and leave to dry on a piece of paper towel.

Arrange the leaves in a single layer on a baking sheet and place in an oven at 350°F (180°C) for around five minutes until the leaves are crispy, but not brown.

Leave to cool completely then crumble a little with your fingers. Combine equal parts celery leaves and sea salt into an airtight jar and stir lightly to combine.

- Rosemary Oil -

---

2 sprigs rosemary
2 cups (500 ml) extra virgin olive oil
5 peppercorns (optional)

Lightly bruise the rosemary by rubbing or rolling the sprigs in your hand to release their aromatic oils. This will bring out their scent and, later, flavor. Add these, and the peppercorns if using, to the olive oil.

Pour into a clean jar or bottle, seal, and leave in a cool dark place for about two weeks to infuse.

Then use as desired, for example over roasted vegetables and/or potatoes.

- IRONING TIPS -

ᔐ Create a distraction or rewards system: Set up your ironing board in front of the TV or treat yourself to a chocolate truffle every time you complete a pile.

ᔐ Heavy pants, cords, or jeans can be shaken from the washing machine and straightened by hand while still damp, then stretched over the back of a chair or hung over a door overnight to dry.

ᔐ Never let anything sit in the dryer after it has finished. If you take everything out when it is still warm and fold it up neatly, most things will not need ironing. Hang shirts straight onto hangers, leave to air, and you'll be surprised how little pressing they actually require.

ᔐ Cheat when ironing bed linen—don't bother with the under-sheet at all and only press the side of the pillowcase and duvet cover that can be seen.

ᔐ To prevent wrinkles forming on areas you have already ironed, keep moving freshly ironed sections away from you.

ᔐ If you don't have a sleeve board, insert a rolled-up towel in sleeves so they can be pressed without leaving creases. Or make your own sleeve board from a cardboard tube covered with soft fabric.

ᔐ To avoid flattening embroidery or eyelets when ironing, iron them facedown on a thick towel.

ᔐ To keep from giving your wash-and-wear garments a sheen when you do touch-up ironing, turn the clothing inside out and iron the wrong side.

- Garlic and Sage Stuffing -

$\frac{1}{3}$ CUP (85 G) BUTTER
1 MEDIUM ONION, FINELY CHOPPED
3 GOOD SIZED GARLIC CLOVES, CRUSHED
1 BEATEN EGG
2$\frac{1}{3}$ CUPS (115 G) BREADCRUMBS (WHITE OR WHOLEMEAL)
1 TABLESPOON OF CHOPPED FRESH SAGE
GRATED ZEST OF LEMON (OPTIONAL)
SALT AND PEPPER

Makes approximately 8 servings

Melt the butter in a saucepan. Then sweat the onions slowly in the pan for about ten minutes until they are soft and translucent but not brown.

Add the crushed garlic and cook for another couple of minutes. Then remove from the heat.

Add the egg, breadcrumbs, sage, and lemon zest if using. Then mix well, and season with salt and pepper.

Finally, use the mixture to stuff the cavity of a bird (chicken, turkey, or goose) before cooking it.

Alternatively, roll it into balls and fry gently with a good dollop of butter or some olive oil for 5 to 6 minutes. If not being used immediately, the stuffing balls can be heated in the oven when you're ready to enjoy them.

- CARVING A TURKEY -

Make sure you have a sharp knitfe and always wear an apron—not only will it protect your clothes, but you'll also need to wipe your hands occasionally.

Stand with the platter turned so that the bird's legs are pointing to your right.

Using a fork to steady the turkey, cut down between the leg and the breast, finding the thigh joint. Cut off the leg and thigh at the joint. Repeat for the other leg. On a separate plate, cut the leg from the thigh.

Cut off the wings by slicing down between the wing and the breast, at the joint.

Carve the breast, slicing from the outside toward the breastbone in long, thin pieces. Then turn the platter and repeat from the other side.

- STOCKING YOUR PANTRY -

In addition to the fresh produce you buy regularly, keep a variety of dried food in the pantry, such as pasta, rice, and assorted dried fruits. Then you will never be caught short when it comes to putting a good meal on the table. A selection of dried herbs is also useful.

Don't turn up your nose at convenience food like canned goods. There are some excellent products available now in cans, such as a variety of beans and fruits, which have a long shelf life, and will always come in handy (canned meat is never a good idea though).

Try to remember to replace items after you use them, so that you always have them in stock for the next meal.

- FIVE SPICE MIXTURE -

---

2 TABLESPOONS BLACK OR SICHUAN PEPPERCORNS
3 STAR ANISE
2 CINNAMON STICKS
5 OR 6 WHOLE CLOVES
2 TEASPOONS FENNEL SEEDS

Toast the peppercorns in a small, heavy, dry pan over a medium heat for
1 or 2 minutes until they become fragrant. Shake the pan frequently as you do
so to prevent burning.

Transfer the toasted peppercorns to a bowl and set aside to cool.

Repeat the toasting process with each of the other ingredients in turn.

Combine the toasted spices and grind* to a fine powder.

Transfer the powder to a glass container, seal it tightly, and store in a cool, dark
place for up to one month.

*NOTE: You may wish to invest in an electric grinder. Otherwise, crack them
by placing them in a freezer bag on a cutting board and pounding with the
bottom of a heavy pan. Or revert to the traditional mortar and pestle.

- MAKING A BED -

A well-made bed can make even the most cluttered of rooms feel much more orderly. First, lay down the bottom sheet: If fitted, just pull tightly over the corners, smoothing from the center, then tuck under the sides; if flat, smoothly tuck in the ends of the sheet and then move on to the corners.

Place your index finger on the corner of the bed and take hold of the sheet hanging down the side with your other hand, about 12–14 inches (30–35 cm) from the foot of the bed, lifting it as you do to form a triangular drape at the corner.

Tuck this drape smoothly under the side of the mattress so that the folded edge of what remains of the hanging sheet forms a 45-degree angle with the corner of the bed. Tuck the rest of the hanging sheet under the mattress, working your way to the other end of the bed. Repeat on all four corners, smoothing any surface wrinkles as you go.

Next, add the top sheet, with the good side facing down and the top aligning with the head of the mattress, so that any extra length falls at the bottom end. Add a blanket on top if desired, good side up, with the top at the point where you'll turn down your top sheet.

Tuck in the bottom edge of both the top sheet and blanket, making sure that you smooth (rather than bunch) them under the mattress. Tuck in the corners as you did for the bottom sheet.

Fold down the top sheet over the top edge of the blanket so that the good side of the sheet is now showing.

Finally, add your duvet and place fluffed up pillows at the head of the bed.

NOTE: It's a good idea to use pillow protectors under your pillow covers to keep them as fresh as possible, and a mattress protector under the bottom sheet.

- MAKING SCENTED CANDLES -

WICK (TWICE THE HEIGHT OF CONTAINER) & WICK TAB
DOUBLE BOILER, OR SAUCEPAN AND HEATPROOF BOWL
CONTAINER WAX
CANDLE DYE DISCS (OPTIONAL)
ESSENTIAL OILS (OPTIONAL)
HEATPROOF CONTAINER, SUCH AS JAM JAR OR CHINA CUP
PENCIL
ADHESIVE PUTTY

Place wick through tab, close tab, and trim off wick.

Put a little water in the lower saucepan and bring to a simmer. Place wax into the top pan or bowl, stirring until melted. At this stage, add the candle dye for color and the essential oils for scent, if desired, stirring to mix evenly.

Pour a tiny bit of melted wax into your container and secure wick in the bottom center. Allow to set, then place an old pencil across the center of your container, attaching it with adhesive putty, and secure the wick vertically to the pencil, ensuring it is straight.

Pour the rest of the melted wax into the container, avoiding the pencil and leaving a little wax to top up your candle as it dips later. Leave to harden for an hour or so. Then top it up with the remaining melted wax and let cool again.

Remove the pencil and trim the wick to about half an inch (1 cm). Leave your new candle for at least several hours before lighting it.

- MAKING BEESWAX POLISH -

A TABLET OF BEESWAX
A GRATER
A LARGE HEATPROOF BOWL
OLIVE OIL OR TURPENTINE
A SAUCEPAN
LEMON ESSENTIAL OIL (OPTIONAL)

Grate a decent amount of the beeswax into a large, heatproof bowl. Grating it speeds up the melting process. (Avoid cross-contamination with food by using a separate grater from your kitchen one.)

Add enough olive oil or turpentine (fermented sap of pine trees) to just cover the wax.

Place the bowl inside a saucepan of simmering (not boiling) water until the ingredients melt and blend together; never heat these ingredients directly*.

Remove from the heat and, if desired, add a few drops of lemon essential oil for a fresh, vibrant scent.

Once the mixture is cool, it can be used straightaway to polish any type of wood or wooden surface, sealing and protecting it. Alternatively the mixture can be stored in an airtight container, away from direct sunlight, for later use.

* NOTE: If the idea of heating the mixture makes you nervous, instead add the ingredients to a sealable jar and simply place it in a warm spot in your home to see if it melts this way.

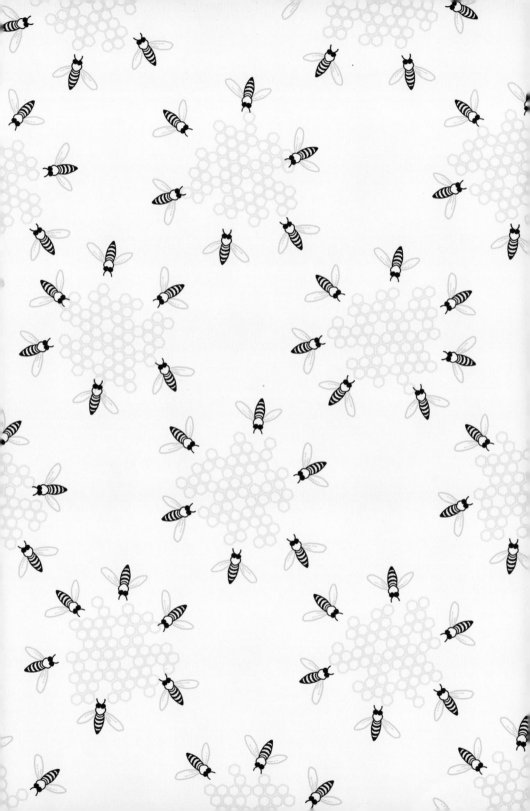

- NOURISHING CHICKEN NOODLE SOUP -

3 TABLESPOONS OF OLIVE OIL
1 SMALL ONION
3 STICKS CELERY
$\frac{1}{2}$ CUP (120 G) CARROTS
6 CUPS (1.5 LITERS) CHICKEN STOCK
$1\frac{2}{3}$ CUPS (400 ML) VEGETABLE STOCK
1 CUP (225 G) SKINLESS, BONELESS CHICKEN BREAST, CHOPPED
$\frac{1}{4}$ CUP (50 G) EGG NOODLES
A PINCH OF DRIED BASIL
A PINCH OF DRIED OREGANO
A BUNCH OF FRESH PARSLEY
SEA SALT AND FRESHLY GROUND BLACK PEPPER

Makes approximately 6 servings

Chop up the onion, celery, and carrots. In a large saucepan, over a medium heat, fry the onion in the oil until it's translucent, then add the celery and cook for a further five minutes.

Pour in the chicken and vegetable stock (fresh stock is best, but a good quality stock cube would work just as well), then stir in the carrots, chicken, noodles, and dried herbs.

Bring to a boil then reduce to a simmer for 20 minutes.

Before serving, season to taste and add the chopped, fresh parsley.

- STORAGE TIPS -

Adequate storage is imperative if you are not to live in chaos. Finding a place for everything requires just a little thought.

❧ Fold a complete set of bed linen (duvet cover and sheet) into the matching pillow case(s), so that it's easy to find when you next go to change the bedding.

❧ Put spare linen in old drawers, then add castors and slide them under the bed.

❧ Run up a few simple drawstring bags and hang them on the back of doors for items you want to have handy, depending on what room you are in, such as scarves, toys, potatoes, or shoe-cleaning equipment.

❧ Make unusual shelving with distressed old floorboards propped up on house-bricks for all your novels. Or use old wooden wine crates.

❧ Plastic vacuum packs save space when storing bulky items such as spare duvets and winter coats, as they will slide neatly under the bed or on a shelf in your closet.

❧ Available in all shapes and sizes, baskets are useful methods of storage. Put them in bathrooms for cosmetics, in the sitting room for current newspapers, in the kids' room for their toys, in the kitchen for fresh vegetables. You might also want to keep an "anything goes" basket into which you can bundle all loose items for a quick tidy at any point. Then once a week simply sort out the contents and return things to their rightful place.

- CLASSIC CHEESE SAUCE -

---

2 TABLESPOONS (25 G) BUTTER
2 TABLESPOONS (25 G) PLAIN FLOUR
2½ CUPS (600 ML) MILK
A PINCH OF SALT, WHITE PEPPER,
AND NUTMEG (OPTIONAL)
¾ CUP (80 G) HARD CHEESE
(SUCH AS CHEDDAR), GRATED

Place the butter in a saucepan and heat until melted.

Stir in the flour with a wire whisk and cook for 1 to 2 minutes.

Take the pan off the heat and gradually stir in the milk, using the whisk to smooth out any lumps. Return to the heat and, stirring continuously, bring to a boil.

Lower the heat and simmer gently for 6 to 10 minutes until the mixture thickens, then season with salt, white pepper, and nutmeg if desired.

Slowly and gradually stir in the cheese(s) of your choice until melted.

Your sauce should now be ready to use, whether with cauliflower, in lasagne or macaroni and cheese, over potatoes, or anything else you fancy.

- LAYING A TABLE -

❧   Lay the cutlery in the order they will be used, working from the outside in—knives and spoons to the right, forks to the left. The blades of the knives should face toward the plate. Dessert spoons and forks can be laid above the plate.

❧   Glasses should be placed on the right-hand side, and also placed in the order that they will be used, from left to right, if you are serving several wines.

❧   Place the side plate to the left of the setting, with a butter knife on top.

❧   Use cloth napkins, particularly if it is a special dinner. They can be folded into the wine glass, slid through a decorative napkin ring, or placed on the side plate or in the center of the setting.

- ALL-NATURAL SURFACE CLEANERS -

❧   Kitchen and bathroom surfaces: Add $1/2$ cup washing soda crystals to 1 gallon (4 liters) warm water.

❧   Refrigerator: Mix 4 tablespoons baking soda with 4 cups (1 liter) warm water.

❧   Windows and glass: Mix white vinegar and water, half and half.

❧   Rinse and dry the surface with a soft cloth at the end for a sparkling finish (or with crumpled newspaper for windows and glass, if preferred).

NOTE: Be sure to label all containers clearly. And always test your product on a small, hidden area before going any further.

- CREAMY VANILLA ICE CREAM -

---

4 EGGS (SEPARATED)
$\frac{1}{2}$ CUP (110 G) SUGAR
$1\frac{1}{4}$ CUPS (300 ML) WHIPPING CREAM
VANILLA EXTRACT

Makes approximately 4 servings

Whisk the egg yolks in a bowl until they are blended.

Whisk the egg whites in a separate, larger bowl, either by hand or using an electric mixer, until they form soft peaks.

Whisk the sugar in with the egg whites, a teaspoon at a time. The whites will get stiffer as the sugar is added.

Blend in the egg yolks until no streaks or color remain.

Whisk the cream until it forms soft peaks and then fold into mixture.

Add a few drops of vanilla extract. Pour mixture into a large plastic container, cover, and freeze.

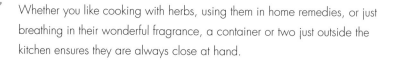

- GROWING HERBS -

Whether you like cooking with herbs, using them in home remedies, or just breathing in their wonderful fragrance, a container or two just outside the kitchen ensures they are always close at hand.

Herbs will grow in almost any container, as long as there is plenty of drainage, so choosing one is simply a matter of personal taste. Choosing which herbs to grow will depend on your intended use for them. For cooking, you might choose from bay, basil, chives, oregano, parsley, sage, tarragon, mint, and thyme. For fragrance, perhaps lavender, lemon verbena, mint, or rosemary.

Don't be afraid to pack your plants in tightly. They will look better and, as long as you prune and water them regularly and bring them indoors for the winter, they will grow well.

Start off by placing some crocks—broken bits of terracotta flowerpots, small stones, or gravel—at the bottom of your container. This will help with drainage. Then fill with potting soil, stopping about 1–2 inches (3–5 cm) from the top.

Remove each plant from its plastic pot by gently squeezing it and teasing out the roots.

Use a trowel to dig a hole in your newly laid soil, carefully place each plant where you want it, and use your hands or the trowel to firm up the soil around each one. Top up with more soil if necessary.

Water your herbs and position them in a sunny spot. The amount of water they need varies depending on the type of herb and where it is being kept, so check the containers regularly and water them if the soil feels dry to the touch.

- CREATING A WINTER WREATH -

A WREATH FORM
SOME EVERGREEN FRONDS
A PAIR OF PRUNING SHEARS
FLORIST'S WIRE
ANY EXTRA DECORATIVE ITEMS YOU WANT

Obtain an inexpensive willow, vine, or straw wreath form from a florist. This will be the frame on which you construct your ring of winter greenery.

Gather some slender, supple fronds from the branch tips of evergreen trees. Cedar, firs, pines, holly, and juniper branches can all be used. Remove them carefully with pruning shears. Never remove greenery from a conservation or protected area. If no winter greenery is available nearby, ask at a Christmas tree wholesaler and they will often give you any broken or discarded branches they wish to dispose of.

Trim the evergreen fronds into small lengths of 6 inches (15 cm) or so.

Lay the wreath form on a table. Then begin attaching the fronds to the form by pushing their ends into the twiggy structure and twisting them around it where necessary.

Add fronds all around the wreath form until it creates a dense, bushy ring of greenery. Use florist's wire to secure any stray fronds.

Finally, add decorations such as winter berries (make sure they're non-toxic), ribbons, bows, or mock presents, binding them on with florist's wire here and there.

- SPRING-CLEANING TIPS -

Some household chores can be tackled just a couple of times a year. The following should fall into your big spring clean checklist:

❧ Carpets: Your carpets require an annual deep-clean—see page 76.

❧ Soft furnishings: A thorough annual cleaning of items such as curtains and loose covers on sofas and armchairs gives them a whole new lease on life (check the care labels to see if these need to be dry-cleaned).

❧ Walls: A gentle circular rubbing with a soft damp cloth and some kitchen cleanser should eradicate dirty marks on light colored paint but watch out for colored wallpaper if you are using a particularly astringent cleaning fluid. Even more effective is a child's pencil eraser.

- FOLDING A SHIRT -

First, button up the shirt—folding an unbuttoned shirt will quickly destroy its shape.

Lay it buttoned-side down on a flat surface, then fold each of the sleeves back, so that they meet in the middle.

Fold one side of the shirt lengthwise to the midpoint of the back. Repeat on the other side.

Fold the bottom upwards to the collar, about a third to half of the way up the length.

Flip the shirt over and neaten up the collar.

- POLISHING WOOD FLOORS -

Polishing will make an old, tired wooden floor look shiny and new. It will also safeguard your wood from future damage by creating a protective barrier between it and any spillages. In a room that doesn't get much foot traffic, polishing should only be required every six to nine months. Be sure, however, that the product you choose is safe for your type of flooring before you begin.

First, remove all furniture from the area to be cleaned and sweep or vacuum to remove all loose dirt. This has abrasive qualities so it can cause nasty scuffs and scratches.

Then clean with a wood floor product, rinse, and dry. Remember to use a damp mop, not a wet one.

Next, starting in the far corner of the room, apply your chosen wax polish with a soft cloth, one small area at a time, and let the wax soak in.

Then simply buff to a nice shine, area by area, with a clean, soft cloth.

To maintain the newly polished effect, sweep the floor regularly—preferably daily—and mop once a week.

Also buff it up now and again using either soft cloths or a broom with a cloth beneath it.

NOTE: If your floor has been polished before and is showing signs of wax build-up, you'll need to get your hands on a wax stripper and follow the instructions advised before applying any new layers of polish.

- Putting Together Potpourri -

FOR APPEARANCE: DRIED FLOWERS, LEAVES, CONES,
AND FRUIT SLICES
FOR A FRAGRANCE: SPICES AND A FEW DROPS OF
ESSENTIAL OIL(S)
A FIXATIVE: SUCH AS CHOPPED, DRIED ORRIS ROOT

First, select your ingredients (some can be bought pre-dried but you may wish to pick and dry others yourself), and then mix together in a large bowl until you're happy with both the look and scent. Enjoy experimenting with this.

Transfer the mix to a sealable jar, close the lid, and leave in a cool, dark place for several weeks to let the scents infuse and intensify. Stir every few days and check the aroma's progress—if the scent isn't strong enough for your liking, add a drop more of your chosen oil(s) and leave for longer.

When ready, arrange your potpourri in a decorative bowl or basket. Then place it wherever you most want a subtle touch of aromatherapy in your home.

If the scent fades with time, add another drop or two of the essential oil(s) and stir to refresh.

Possible combinations

WARM & SPICY: Dried, chopped orris root. Dried orange slices. Whole cloves. Cinnamon sticks. Sweet orange or ylang ylang oil.

LIGHT & ZESTY: Dried, chopped orris root or dried lavender. Dried lemon slices. Dried rose petals. Dried geranium leaves. Lemon or lavender oil.

- FIVE USES FOR VINEGAR -

❀ To clean windows and mirrors: Mix half white vinegar and half water in a spray bottle, then spray and wipe with a dry cloth or piece of newspaper.

❀ To prevent limescale build-up in your dishwasher: Put white vinegar in the tablet dispenser and run it on a normal wash once a month.

❀ To remove tea and coffee stains: Place a teaspoon of white vinegar and a pinch of salt in the vessel. Wipe with a damp cloth, then wash as normal.

❀ To soothe an insect sting or bite: Dab the affected area with a cotton ball soaked in white vinegar (which has anti-inflammatory properties).

❀ To clean burnt pots: Boil 2 tablespoons of vinegar in a little water for 5 to 10 minutes, then empty and scrape off the burnt bits with a wooden utensil.

- FIVE USES FOR BAKING SODA -

❀ To prevent clogged drains: Pour $1/4-1$ cup baking soda down the sink weekly and rinse with hot water.

❀ To "destink" smelly shoes: Sprinkle powder into the offending footwear, leave overnight, then shake out; the same trick works for stale-smelling bins.

❀ To eliminate odors from soft furnishings, including carpets: Generously sprinkle powder onto the affected areas, leave for at least fifteen minutes, and vacuum off.

❀ To freshen up your refrigerator: Place an open bowl of baking soda in the refrigerator for as long as it takes to neutralize unpleasant odors.

❀ For a more effective wash: Add $1/2$ cup baking soda to your usual amount of laundry detergent to get "whiter whites" and brighter colors.

- SHARPENING A KNIFE -

All straight-edge knives should be sharpened regularly to get the best results when slicing and dicing. Sharp knives make food preparation not only faster and easier but also safer: You need to apply less pressure, which means there's less chance of the knife slipping.

In an ideal world, household knives should be sharpened on a device called a steel at least once a week.

Make sure your knife is clean and dry. Hold the steel vertically, tip down on a chopping board. Then stroke the knife's blade downward, at an angle of approximately 20 degrees, an equal amount of times on each side (between 6 and 10 should do the trick).

Go slowly for safety's sake: Accuracy of angle is more important than speed as you don't want to damage the sides of your knife (or your hand!). If you don't feel confident, it's best to send your knives off to be professionally sharpened.

When honing your knife on a steel no longer gives you the sharp edge desired, it's time to move onto a whetstone. Buy a high quality stone from a reliable company that can offer you advice on how to use it. A good stone will last a lot longer than a cheap one and will be a lot less frustrating to use.

NOTE: Always chop on a wooden or plastic surface; glass and ceramic surfaces are too hard on the blade. Never put your good knives in the dishwasher.

- SEWING A SAMPLER -

Samplers were made before the days of pattern books; women would record new stitches by sewing samples onto pieces of cloth.

These days kits to make them are available in craft stores and on the Internet. These contain all you need to make your own: fabric, needles, threads, the sampler design of your choice, the stitch chart to follow, and stitching guidelines for beginners.

It's best to start with a kit that is completely pre-designed for you so that you simply need to follow the steps given.

If you're a beginner, choose a kit that involves just one type of stitch, such as cross-stitch, for ease. Then progress to ones with more variety—eyelet, feather, herringbone…. Always try out new stitches on spare fabric first if you are unsure of them.

Once you become more confident, you can proceed to kits that give you more independence with your design. At this stage, you'll need some graph paper to chart your plan before you get stitching.

You can create a sampler around any theme, whether the alphabet, floral or animal designs, geometric patterns, a recent event such as a birth or marriage, your family tree, or a positive message, such as the classic "Home Sweet Home."

- TRADITIONAL HOT TODDY -

A STRONG SPIRIT (MOST COMMONLY WHISKEY*)
HOT WATER
1-2 SPOONFULS OF HONEY
$\frac{1}{2}$-1 LEMON SLICE
A FEW CLOVES (OPTIONAL)
ALLSPICE OR A CINNAMON STICK (OPTIONAL)

Half fill a glass with just-boiled water. Placing a spoon in the glass and pouring the water over it will help to prevent the glass cracking from the heat; otherwise heat your glass slightly before adding the water.

Stir in a spoonful or two of honey.

Add half a lemon slice with 2–4 cloves inserted into it. If you want a strong citrus flavor, squeeze in the juice of the other half of the lemon slice.

If desired, add a pinch of allspice or a cinnamon stick for extra kick.

Finally add a good glug of the whiskey to taste, give it a stir, and you're ready to go.

*NOTE: There's no point breaking out your best single malt for this winter warmer as the subtle flavors would be wasted.

- REPAINTING WOOD FURNITURE -

Before you start trying to breathe fresh life into old pieces of furniture, spend some time investigating the types of paints available and what effect you would like to achieve. Look in design magazines for inspiration. Always experiment on inexpensive pieces before working on anything more valuable.

Don your old clothes or overalls and cover the flooring.

Remove all handles from the item in question.

Rub it down, using fine sandpaper, until there are no shiny or flaky surfaces left. Then wipe away any dust.

Fill any holes with wood filler and touch them up with primer.

If you want a vintage effect, rub a candle on the areas where the paint would most likely be worn on an old piece of furniture; make a note of where you've done this.

Then begin painting: Start with the details, using a small brush (including any undersides, lips, nooks and crannies); then the legs; and finally large, flat panels, one at a time.

Be sure to let each coat dry before applying the next: first a primer, then an undercoat, finally a topcoat of eggshell, satin, or gloss.

If you applied wax to certain areas for a vintage effect, now rub the same areas with fine sandpaper or wire wool.

Finally, replace all handles and you're done.

- POLISHING SHOES -

To keep leather shoes looking their best, they should be polished regularly—preferably once a week but at least once a month. Wax polish gives the best shine, while cream polish will allow the leather to breathe more.

First wash off any surplus dirt with a damp cloth and let your shoes dry naturally, helping to maintain their natural shape by stuffing crumpled newspaper into the toes or inserting shoe trees.

Once the leather is dry, dab a small amount of the appropriate color shoe polish onto a cloth or shoe brush and rub over each shoe using small, circular movements. Make sure you get into any creases and the section between the upper and sole. Allow the polish to soak into the leather for at least ten minutes. Then vigorously buff with a clean cloth or shoe brush to achieve the desired shine.

- WASHING CASHMERE -

Gently hand-washing some cashmere garments can prolong their life, but be sure to check the care instructions on the label before beginning.

Choose a detergent suitable for fine fabrics. Make sure to use the recommended amount of detergent and water temperature (usually either cool or lukewarm).

Submerge your garment in the soapy water, gently moving the suds through the fabric without rubbing. Then rinse your garment until the water runs clear.

Lay the garment on a clean, dry towel, roll up the towel and press with your palms to squeeze out the excess water, then smooth the garment out on a clean, flat surface to let it dry naturally. Never hang or tumble dry cashmere.

- PERFECT PANCAKES -

---

1 EGG
1¹/₄ CUPS (280 ML) MILK
³/₄ CUP (110 G) ALL-PURPOSE FLOUR
A PINCH OF SALT
1 TABLESPOON OIL, SUCH AS VEGETABLE
OR SUNFLOWER OIL
TOPPINGS OF YOUR CHOICE

Makes approximately 8 pancakes

In a large bowl, whisk the egg into the milk.

Put the flour and salt in a mixing bowl, and gradually add the egg and milk mixture, stirring vigorously to remove lumps. The finished batter should be runny and creamy.

Add a drop of oil to a heavy-based frying pan and place on the stove at a high heat. Add two large spoonfuls of batter and tilt the pan until it is thinly but evenly coated.

The first side only takes about 1 minute to cook. When it's done, flip the pancake and cook the other side.

Then place on a plate and add the toppings of your choice.

- GROWING CHILI PEPPERS -

The key things to remember when growing chili peppers are that they like to stay nice and warm, and they don't like to be overwatered.

Choose your desired variety of seeds and plant them in plug pots (small trays divided into little squares) in early spring: Fill each pot with potting soil, insert a seed, and lightly cover with soil.

Spray with water to avoid over-soaking and cover with a plastic lid or saran wrap to create a mini greenhouse effect.

Keep in a warm, dark place such as the pantry or a cupboard. Check each day, but many start to sprout in 7 to 10 days.

Once they have started to germinate, move them to another warm place, but this time with plenty of light, such as on a sunny windowsill; bring them away from windows at night or the drop in temperature may kill them.

When the seedlings grow to about 3–4 inches (8–10 cm), move them into individual pots about 3–4 inches (8–10 cm) in diameter and place them in a sunny, sheltered outside spot. They will need to be outdoors by the time flowers appear to enable insects to do the pollinating for you, which will create the recognizable fruits.

Transplant them into bigger pots several times as they grow, finishing in a pot approximately 8 inches (20 cm) in diameter and watering as required—the soil should never feel too wet.

Feed them with half-strength diluted liquid feed once or twice a week at first, then daily when the much-anticipated fruit starts to appear.

- REMOVING STAINS -

Always tackle stains immediately—the longer you leave them the harder they will be to get out. Scrape up any surface matter before you start and blot as much of the stain away as you can. Do not rub it—this will only spread it. And always work from the outside of the stain in. For specific stains, try the following:

BLOOD: Soak immediately in cold water—never hot.

CANDLE WAX: Leave the wax to solidify, then gently scrape off as much as you can with a blunt, flat-edged knife. Lay a sheet of grease-proof paper over (and if possible under) the mark and dry-iron on the lowest temperature.

CHEWING GUM: Place the item in the freezer. Once hard, the gum should come off easily. Then wash as usual. This also works for chocolate.

RED & WHITE WINE: Soak in soda water immediately, followed by the hottest wash the care label allows. This also works for tea and coffee stains.

BALLPOINT PEN: Dab with a cotton pad soaked in rubbing alcohol, then wash as normal, or rub the stain gently using an eraser to fade the mark.

COOKING OIL OR FAT: Sprinkle with talcum powder and leave for 30 minutes. Then brush off and wash as normal.

MILDEW: Take the item outside and remove surface mildew with a stiff brush. Leave to air in the sun. If spots remain, wash in biological detergent.

RUST: Douse with salt, then pour lemon juice over and put the garment in the sun. A small mark should fade after a few hours, a heavier mark may take days.

PERSPIRATION: Sponge underarm perspiration with white wine vinegar, rinse then wash as usual.

- WHOLESOME MUESLI -

3 CUPS (300 G) ROLLED OATS
1 CUP (100 G) MIXED NUTS INCLUDING
MACADAMIAS, FLAKED ALMONDS, AND WALNUTS
4 TABLESPOONS ($\frac{1}{4}$ CUP) EACH OF SESAME SEEDS,
SUNFLOWER SEEDS, PUMPKIN SEEDS, RAISINS,
DRIED CRANBERRIES, AND COCONUT FLAKES
A HANDFUL (1 CUP) DRIED APRICOTS, CHOPPED

Mix all the ingredients together in a large bowl, then decant into a large, air-tight container.

Serve with fresh chopped fruit, a dollop of yogurt, and a drizzle of honey.

- APPLE SAUCE -

2 CUPS (500 G) CHOPPED APPLES
THE ZEST OF A LEMON
2 TABLESPOONS SUPERFINE SUGAR
CINNAMON STICK
4 TABLESPOONS WATER
4 TABLESPOONS BUTTER
A PINCH OF SALT

Place all the ingredients in a saucepan, cover, and cook on a low heat until the apples are soft and mushy—around 10 minutes.

Remove the pan from the heat and discard the cinnamon stick before serving. (Can be kept in the refrigerator for a week or in the freezer for up to a year.)

- REFRESHING CRANBERRY JUICE -

4$\frac{1}{2}$ CUPS (450 G) CRANBERRIES
5 CUPS (1.2 LITERS) WATER
A PINCH OF SALT
3 ORANGE SLICES (OPTIONAL)
$\frac{1}{2}$ CUP (100 G) SUGAR

Makes approximately 8 servings

Wash the cranberries and put them into a saucepan with the water,
salt and, if you wish, the orange slices.

Cook on the stove over medium heat until all the berries burst.
This should take about 10 minutes.

Pour the fruit and liquid into a cheesecloth-lined sieve, and strain
the juice back into the saucepan.

Add the sugar and boil for two or three minutes.
Taste and add more sugar if it is needed.

Cool and chill the juice before serving.

- SEASONAL STORAGE -

When the temperatures start to shift, marking the start of a new season, it's time to sort clothes for the months ahead:

❧ Empty your wardrobe and sell or give away anything that no longer fits, looks worn out, or that you no longer like.

❧ Wash and thoroughly dry all other garments. Any small stains or minor odors can really set in over time, which is likely to attract household pests such as moths and other insects.

❧ Fold or hang up any items that you are likely to wear in the season ahead and set aside the rest for storage.

❧ Plastic vacuum packs are particularly useful for storing winter woolens such as cashmere sweaters—not only because they save space but also because moths prefer nibbling on natural fibers.

❧ Transparent plastic boxes with tight-fitting lids are also useful but it's advisable to disinfect and line them with a cotton sheet or acid-free tissue before adding clothing. Stack clothes loosely to allow ventilation.

- GRANDMA'S APPLE PIE -

1 CUP (225 G) BUTTER, ROOM TEMPERATURE
1/4 CUP (50 G) GOLDEN SUPERFINE SUGAR
2 EGGS
3 CUPS (360 G) PLAIN FLOUR
2 LBS (1 KG) APPLES
3/4 CUP (150 G) GOLDEN SUPERFINE SUGAR
3 TABLESPOONS FLOUR
A PINCH OF CINNAMON, NUTMEG, AND ALLSPICE

To make the pastry, beat the butter and sugar together until just mixed, then add one whole egg and the yolk from the other (save the white). Beat the mixture until it starts to resemble scrambled egg—this should take about a minute.

Now add the flour, in three parts, stirring with a wooden spoon to combine. It will begin to form a ball, so help it along with your hands, then wrap it in saran wrap and let chill for 45 minutes.

While your dough chills, peel and core your apples, then chop into bite-size pieces. Place on paper towel to soak up any juices, then put into a large bowl, add the sugar, flour, and spices, and mix lightly with your fingers.

Heat your oven to 375°F (190°C), then roll out two thirds of your pastry to generously line a pie tin 8-inches (20-cm) in diameter.

Toss your apples into the pie tin, brush the edge of the pastry with a bit of water to help create a seal, then roll out the rest of your pastry, lay over the apples, and pinch around the edge to seal. Trim off the excess pastry and make a few slits in the lid to let steam escape.

Brush with the leftover egg white and sprinkle with sugar, then bake for 45 minutes until the pastry is golden.

- GIFT-WRAPPING TIPS -

A neatly wrapped parcel makes a gift even more special as the recipient can tell that time, energy, and effort has been put into its creation. Here are some tips to help you on your way to the wrapping success that so many find elusive.

↬ Remember to remove price tags before you begin.

↬ Consider placing the gift inside a box if it's an awkward shape to make it easier to wrap.

↬ Be mindful of how much wrapping paper you use. You want enough to cover the gift but not so much that it becomes bulky. It should go around the box lengthwise with about 2 inches (5 cm) of overlap and you don't need much at each end.

↬ If the gift is cylinder-shaped, try rolling the wrapping paper around it, with a little overlap in the middle, and scrunching the ends to create a "cracker" shape, then securing each end with a ribbon.

↬ Create a "hem" of folded-in paper on all visible wrapping paper edges for the neatest possible finish—this will prevent any messily cut raw edges from showing on your finished product.

↬ Try using a Scotch pop-up tape dispenser with elastic wristband, which delivers small, readymade strips of the sticky stuff, thus saving you from having to awkwardly juggle the scissors, sticky tape, and gift, as well as saving you from constantly losing your place on the sticky tape.

↬ Always decorate gifts with a ribbon or bow, and don't forget a gift card.

- SAVORY PIE CRUST -

---

1 CUP (125 G) PLAIN FLOUR
A PINCH OF SALT
$1/4$ CUP (55 G) BUTTER, CUBED
2–3 TABLESPOONS COLD WATER

In a large bowl, combine the flour and salt, then add the cubes of butter. Using your fingers (cold hands are best), rub together the butter and flour so that the mixture resembles breadcrumbs. Work quickly so that the mixture does not become too warm and greasy.

Add the cold water a spoonful at a time (you might not need it all), and using a knife, stir the mixture so that it binds together to form a dough.

Once the mixture has come together, form into a ball of dough with your hands, wrap in saran wrap, and put in the refrigerator to chill for at least 15 minutes.

To blind bake, heat your oven to 375°F (190°C). Once the dough is chilled, sprinkle a clean surface with flour and roll out your pastry into a circle around $1/8$–$1/4$ inch (0.5 cm) thick. Lift this into a pie dish, with the help of your rolling pin, and make sure the pastry is sitting deep in the base of the dish and hanging over the sides (you'll trim this later).

Prick the pastry with a fork, then place a sheet of parchment paper over it and fill the dish with ceramic pie weights. Bake for 15 minutes, then remove the parchment paper and pie weights and put back into the oven for another five minutes or until the pastry is a light golden brown. Trim the excess pastry once you have added—and baked—your pie filling.

- MAKING A SCRAPBOOK -

Once a year, why not put your memories and keepsakes together in a book? Buy a blank book or album that appeals to you and stick in everything you have saved from memorable occasions.

You might want to add in some written commentaries or photographs of the occasions too—to remind you when, where, and with whom each event took place. Be as creative as you like with what you choose to include and their placement, such as:

- ticket stubs
- business cards or receipts from favorite restaurants or special meals
- the invitation or menu from a special occasion, such as a wedding
- sweet or funny notes that your partner, friends, or family have left for you
- postcards from loved ones
- leaves collected during walks in the fall

- DRYING FRUITS -

Choose ripe fruit in good condition. Wash, peel, and pit or core the fruit if relevant.

Slice it, bearing in mind that thicker slices will take longer to dry. Small, soft fruits such as blueberries, cherries, and apricots, however, should be dried whole.

Place the slices on a baking tray lined with parchment paper, making sure that the slices don't touch one another, and bake in the oven at between 100 and 140°F (40 and 60°C) for several hours, checking every hour or so to see if the fruit needs turning.

Remove from oven once ready (it should end up chewy; not squishy or crunchy). Let it sit for at least 12 hours before storing in airtight jars in a cool, dry place.

- MOTHPROOFING -

To protect your much-loved clothes and household textiles, it's crucial to discourage moths from getting into the cozy spots where they love to lay their eggs. Otherwise, their caterpillar-like larvae will have a feast.

Cedar wood is one of the most effective natural ways to keep them at bay. Simply buy cedar wood blocks or balls and place them in your wardrobes and drawers. Then replace the deterrents every three to six months, regularly checking for any sign of moth activity.

This is especially important when it comes to storing items made from natural fibers such as wool, cashmere, and silk. These are the most susceptible to moth damage due to their high keratin content (the larvae have the unusual ability to digest and use keratin as an energy source). The fact that synthetic fibers tend only to be damaged incidentally makes storage options such as plastic vacuum packs particularly useful—for example to store winter wool sweaters over the summer months.

NOTE: If you've already found suspicious holes in some of your garments, prevent further damage by removing all clothes from the affected wardrobe or drawers. Wash them at the highest temperature recommended on the care labels and thoroughly vacuum not only the interior of the storage unit but also the entire room. Eliminate any eggs or larvae by spraying the unit with an organic moth spray. Deter any further pests with cedar wood products as above.

- DARNING A HOLE -

DARNING NEEDLE
THREAD (MATCH THE YARN TO THE FABRIC
AS CLOSELY AS POSSIBLE)
MUSHROOM (TO HOLD BEHIND THE HOLE TO
CREATE TENSION)

First, darn up and down. Work from the wrong side, starting and finishing a good distance away from the hole, on the "good" part of the fabric—to provide reinforcement. Start by anchoring the thread using one or two running stitches in the fabric at the bottom edge of the hole.

Carry the thread across the gap to the top of the hole and anchor it with a small stitch there.

Criss-cross from top to bottom over the hole, until it is covered with parallel rows of thread.

Then, darn across. Begin to "weave" horizontally over and under alternate strands of your vertical stitching.

This time, only work back and forth over the actual hole, plus a few strands into the thinning sections on each side. In alternate rows, pick up the strands of yarn you passed over in the previous row. This creates the "weave" effect.

Finish off with a few small running stitches through the fabric.

- ARRANGING FLOWERS -

To make a striking floral arrangement, first choose your container accordingly.
All kinds of items can make good "vases"—from bottles, bowls, and baskets to
teapots, old watering cans, and even old walking boots.

Next choose your flowers and foliage. Different shapes, colors, and textures will
make an interesting design but simplicity can sometimes work just as well. You
will need three shapes: "line" material (long, straight stems) to form the structure;
"rounded" material (particularly flowers but also leaves) to act as focal points; and
"filler" material, to "fill" any unwanted gaps and add detail and lightness.

Using flowers in different stages of their development, from bud to full bloom, will
also add variety. And it can be a nice touch to include at least one bloom that
carries personal significance for the recipient of the bouquet.

Allow some space between flowers to prevent over-crowding unless you're going
for a particularly packed-in posy look. Make sure that colors are evenly balanced
throughout. And when using open flowers, such as daffodils and gerbera, try
turning them to face different directions for heightened interest.

Always cut stems at an angle before placing them in the water, and trim off any
leaves below the water's surface.

SIMPLE SUGGESTIONS
- ໑ A cluster of fresh daisies or peonies in glass tumblers.
- ໑ Posies of bright sweet peas in old preserve jars.
- ໑ A couple of carnations in old soup cans (repainted if you've had the time).
- ໑ A single stem in an elegant glass decanter, such as a calla lily or foxglove.
- ໑ A stem of orchids embedded within a cylindrical glass vase.

- CLEANING A CARPET -

The key to keeping carpets clean is regular vacuuming—at least once or twice a week for frequently used areas, and once a month or so beneath furniture.

However, when a run-round with the vacuum no longer does the job, it's time for a deep clean. Many people these days call in the professionals, however, below are some guidelines if you'd rather do it yourself. Most modern carpets are suitable for home-cleaning but always check the care instructions for your own carpet first.

- ❧ Always try a test patch in a discreet area first.

- ❧ Never get the carpet too wet.

- ❧ Vacuum thoroughly to remove as much loose dirt as possible.

- ❧ Treat any bad stains to reduce their visibility to a minimum (see p. 62).

- ❧ If you have access to a carpet-cleaning machine, follow the instructions. Otherwise, start in the back corner of the space to be cleaned and apply a purpose-made solution with a soft scrubbing brush or cloth. Work gently in the direction of the pile, one small area at a time, soaking up any excess moisture with old white towels as you go.

- ❧ Give the carpet plenty of time to dry—warm weather and open windows are the quickest solution. If the room is left unventilated, a damp carpet will soon start to smell.

- ❧ Once the carpet is dry, vacuum to remove any dried-in cleaning agent. This will also help to restore the pile.

- HOMEMADE TOMATO SAUCE -

---

4 TABLESPOONS OF OLIVE OIL
4 CLOVES OF GARLIC
3 x 14 OZ (400 G) CANNED WHOLE PLUM TOMATOES
A BUNCH OF FRESH BASIL, CHOPPED
SEA SALT AND FRESHLY GROUND BLACK PEPPER

Heat the oil in a saucepan. Then peel and finely chop the garlic
and toss into the pan.

Once the garlic has started to soften and deliciously scent the oil,
add the tomatoes and chopped basil. Break up the tomatoes a bit
with a wooden spoon, then season.

Once the tomatoes come to a boil, remove the pan from the heat and strain the
mixture through a strainer, discarding any basil and garlic that's left behind.

Pour the smooth sauce back into the pan, bring to a boil again, then reduce to
a simmer for five minutes.

This sauce will keep for a week in the refrigerator or a month in the freezer.

- TRANSPLANTING HOUSE PLANTS -

Signs that a houseplant needs repotting to a bigger container include top-heaviness, roots peeping out of drainage holes, and the plant's failure to blossom at the normal rate. If possible, do any re-potting in the spring when most plants are starting to "wake up" and think about producing new roots and shoots.

Choose a pot an inch or two (2–4 cm) bigger than the old one.

Place some pieces of broken pots or stones in the bottom of it to improve drainage.

Fill the container about a quarter full with potting soil. It's fine to reuse soil if it looks healthy and bug-free; otherwise, best to opt for new.

Turn the plant upside down with one hand on the soil surface and the stem between your fingers. With your other hand, tap the rim on the edge of a hard surface until the plant loosens.

Shake excess soil from the roots and make sure that they look healthy.

Hold the plant in the center of the new pot and fill soil around it until just below the rim of the pot, firming it down at the top.

Stand the pot in a saucer and water from the bottom with tepid water. If the soil at the top shows signs of damp, tip away any water left in the saucer. Allow the plant to drain before placing back in the saucer.

Keep the plant in its former location if possible until it has settled. This helps to prevent transplant shock.

- QUICK FRUIT SMOOTHIE -

$^2/_3$ CUP (150 ML) VANILLA YOGURT
$^1/_3$ CUP (75 ML) MILK
$^1/_3$ CUP (75 ML) ORANGE JUICE
A HANDFUL OF STRAWBERRIES
1 BANANA
A HANDFUL OF ICE CUBES

Serves 1

Add the liquid ingredients to the blender.

Then add the rest of the ingredients, one at a time, blitzing briefly
(sometimes called pulsing) in between each new addition to avoid
clogging up the blender blade.

Check the consistency of your smoothie. If it's too thick, add more milk.
Too thin, a little more yogurt.

Pour into a tall glass over ice cubes, add a straw, and maybe a strawberry for
decoration if you like, and it's ready to drink.

- FABRIC CARE -

A basic understanding of fabric care is essential in order to avoid washday disasters such as shrinkage, running, pilling, puckering, and rips.

👋 Sort your laundry into four separate piles for washing—whites, lights, coloreds, and delicates/handwash.

👋 Empty all pockets—items such as bank notes and passports are not improved by a run through the wash.

👋 Do up zips, hooks, and fasteners that might snag other clothing or work loose.

👋 Soak or pre-treat any heavily soiled items before washing, or you can end up redistributing dirt onto less soiled items in the machine.

👋 Check the label to see what each garment is made of—cottons can generally withstand higher temperatures, while synthetics need a cooler wash. However, the recommended temperature is usually given on the label.

👋 Some things are better washed inside out—particularly clothing with transfers or embroidery. Jeans will fade less quickly too if you turn them the wrong way round.

👋 Wash delicates separately from heavier fabrics—they fare better that way.

👋 Don't be tempted to overfill the machine—clothes need enough space to be agitated correctly to facilitate the washing process.

👋 Use a mesh bag to wash fragile lingerie and refrain from machine-washing underwired bras. The wires can come loose and snag other clothing.

👋 Don't leave your laundry in the machine for long once the wash cycle is complete. Try to hang it up or put it in the dryer right away.

- HANGING A PICTURE -

First, decide where you want to hang your picture. Then hold it in place, measure halfway along the top edge of the frame and make a pencil mark on the wall.

Choose a picture hook or nail appropriate to the weight of your picture and type of wall. Heavier items may require a screw anchor and screw, which means you'll need to get out your drill. Specialist wallplugs are available for plasterboard walls if needed.

Hold the picture's wire taught at its center and measure from here to the frame's top edge.

Measure the same distance down from the pencil mark on the wall and make another mark.

Either hammer your hook—or drill and screw—into this second mark. Hang your picture and adjust it so it's level.

NOTE: Never hang a picture above or below light switches or electrical sockets. You may wish to invest in a multi-purpose electric tester for safety. This will detect any electric current or metal pipes running behind walls.

- POLISHING SILVER -

To keep silver sparkling it needs to be polished regularly. Wear thin cotton gloves as you work to prevent finger marks being left on the newly gleaming surfaces.

The easiest way to clean small silver items, such as jewelry, is with silver cleaning dip. Simply place the jewelry in the container for the specified time, remove and buff with a clean cloth. Be sure, however, to check before starting whether any precious stones set in your jewelry are safe to be exposed to the solution.

For larger items, place a small amount of liquid silver cleaner on a dry, clean cloth and rub the silver in small, gentle, circular movements. You can tackle any engraved or ridged areas in the same way with an old, soft toothbrush.

As the polish dries, start rubbing with a clean cloth to remove it. When the cloth becomes black, switch to another clean cloth, continuing in this way until your silver is shining. There should be no residue left on your final cloth.

- WRITING A THANK-YOU NOTE -

There's nothing like a little thank you note to ackowledge a gift, event, or any act of kindness, and a handwritten card or letter will almost always seem more thoughtful and give more pleasure than an email.

You don't need to write a lot, but be sure to make what you do write personal. For example, if someone has given you a gift, say specifically why you like it (even if you don't!). You might even want to include a photo of you using it.

If the note is from a couple it's preferable for both people to express their thanks, even if it's just by a simple signing of names.

And remember that time is of the essence: Send your note within two or three days of the act of kindness if possible.

- Everyday Vegetable Stock -

---

2 ONIONS, ROUGHLY CHOPPED
2 CARROTS, CUT INTO CHUNKS
2 CELERY STALKS
1 LEEK
SMALL BUNCH OF PARSLEY STALKS
SPRIG OF THYME
3 PEPPERCORNS
2 GARLIC CLOVES UNPEELED
5-6 PINTS (2.5-3 LITERS) WATER

Put all the ingredients into a large saucepan, and bring to a boil, skimming any scum from the surface. Simmer for about one and a half hours.

Then strain through a sieve and either use immediately, or store in the refrigerator for up to about five days or in the freezer for two to three months.

For Chicken Stock

Halve the amount of vegetables and add two broken-up chicken carcasses (kept either raw or cooked in the freezer) and giblets (optional).

Simmer for double the time, ensuring there is enough water.

Allow to cool and remove the solidified fat from the surface.

- FESTIVE EGGNOG -

4 EGG YOLKS
$\frac{1}{2}$ CUP (100 G) SUGAR
2 CUPS (475 ML) WHOLE MILK
A PINCH OF CINNAMON
1 VANILLA BEAN
1 CUP (237 ML) HEAVY CREAM
$\frac{3}{4}$ CUP (200 ML) BRANDY
1 TEASPOON FRESHLY GRATED NUTMEG

Makes approximately 8 servings

In a large bowl, whisk the egg yolks until they become pale in color, then add the sugar in four parts, beating in between, so the mixture becomes light and fluffy.

Pour the milk into a saucepan and add the cinnamon and vanilla bean. Then warm over a medium heat until the milk goes frothy and is just about to boil.

Remove the milk from the heat and pour a splash of it into the egg mixture, then stir. Add a little more, then stir again, and finally, pour it all in. Adding the milk to the eggs, and not vice versa, means you won't get scrambled eggs!

Pour everything back into the saucepan and return to the heat. Stir constantly until the mixture thickens and coats the back of a wooden spoon (around 10 minutes). Make sure it doesn't boil.

Remove from the heat and discard the vanilla bean. Stir in the heavy cream, let your mixture cool for an hour, then pour in the brandy, and chill.

Sprinkle with freshly grated nutmeg before serving.

- DRYING AND PRESERVING HERBS -

There are many ways to use herbs in the home—whether as decoration, in home spa remedies, in herbal teas, or in delicious culinary creations. Using fresh herbs is often best but it's useful to keep some preserved for when the need arises. There are several ways to do this:

AIR-DRYING: Hang bunches of long-stem herbs upside down in a warm, airy spot and leave for several weeks. Then store the dried leaves and flowers in airtight jars in a dark place.

FREEZING: Loosely pack the leaves of fresh herbs into freezer bags, label for identification, and freeze.

MAKING ICE CUBES: Place chopped herbs in ice cube trays, cover with water, and freeze. Drop the cubes into soups and stews, or add a refreshing mint cube to a glass of water on a hot summer's day.

PRESERVING IN OIL: Immerse entire stems of fresh herbs in olive oil for about a week for use on bread, salads, and the like.

- SERVING HIGH TEA -

High tea is a great way to add a touch of elegance and occasion to an afternoon gathering. The following is a selection of ideas for teatime treats:

∽ Dainty sandwiches, cut into small triangles without crusts. You can make any filling you like, but some common choices are cucumber, egg, or poached salmon.

∽ Fresh scones and a selection of delicious mini cakes, such as fruit cake, macaroons, carrot cake, brownies, and banana bread muffins.

∽ Cream and jam for the scones—ideally served in separate little pots, one of each for every guest if possible.

∽ An assortment of chintzy teapots, china cups (with saucers), milk jug, sugar bowl, and plates. A layered cake stand will make for a lovely presentation.

∽ Stock up on English Breakfast, Earl Grey, peppermint, chamomile, jasmine, and any other varieties that take your fancy. Pink champagne is an optional extra.

- A PERFECT CUP OF TEA -

To make the perfect cup, you must start with good-quality tea, whether loose-leaf or bagged, that has been stored in an airtight container at room temperature.

Make sure to boil the kettle with fresh water each time you want a cup. The best flavor is extracted from the tea leaves when the water contains oxygen— the oxygen levels of the water reduce each time the water is re-boiled.

Allow one tea bag or one rounded teaspoon of loose-leaf tea for each cup, and steep the tea for approximately three minutes—any longer and the tea is likely to be bitter with a bad aftertaste.

- LEMON, GINGER, AND HONEY TEA -

½ INCH (1–2CM) PIECE GINGER, SLICED OR GRATED
1 CUP HOT WATER
JUICE OF HALF A LEMON
1 TABLESPOON HONEY

Place ginger in a tea pot, pour 1 cup freshly boiled water over it and let it steep for about 5 minutes.

Put lemon juice and honey in a mug, then strain the ginger tea into the mug, stirring to dissolve the honey.

- HOT CHOCOLATE -

⅔ CUPS (170 G) CHOPPED CHOCOLATE
2 CUPS (500 ML) MILK

Boil a little water in a saucepan, then turn the heat down to simmer. Place the chocolate into a heat-resistant bowl and place the bowl over the saucepan, making sure it does not touch the bottom. Stir the chocolate occasionally until it has melted into a smooth consistency.

Put the melted chocolate to one side while you heat the milk in a saucepan over a low flame. Keep an eye on the chocolate to make sure it doesn't harden.

Add the chocolate to the milk, mixing well.

- RIPENING TOMATOES -

There are often green tomatoes left on the vine in the autumn that are in danger of succumbing to the frost if growing outside. So how can we get these to ripen?

Green tomatoes can be picked, wrapped individually in newspaper, and placed in a box no more than two layers deep. Then just put the box in a dark, dry spot and check weekly for progress. It usually takes three to four weeks for them to ripen, but check frequently and remove any fruits that show signs of rotting.

An option for more mature green tomatoes (which have a tinge of color at the blossom end and feel a little softer than the solid young fruits) is simply to place them on a sunny inside window sill. This can be a little hit or miss as it depends on how much sunshine you get.

Another option is to place green tomatoes in a brown paper bag with a ripe apple. The apple gives off ethylene gas, which speeds up ripening. Check the bag daily.

Alternatively, instead of picking the unripe tomatoes, you can lift the entire plant out of its potting soil in the garden and place (or hang) it in a dry, sheltered location, like the garage. Try to take some roots with the plant, but shake off any soil. Avoid direct sunlight or total darkness.

- Knitting a Chunky Scarf Collar -

2 SKEINS SIRDAR BIG SOFTIE SUPER CHUNKY
[51% WOOL, 49% ACRYLIC, 49 YDS (45 M)/50 G]
US SIZE 13 (9 MM) STRAIGHT NEEDLES
TAPESTRY NEEDLE

GAUGE

12 stitches and 14 rows = 4 in (10 cm) in pattern

SIZE

16 in (41 cm) circumference x 7 in (18 cm) deep

INSTRUCTIONS

Cast on 48 stitches.

Rows 1–4: knit 2, purl 2; repeat sequence across the row.

Rows 5–8: purl 2, knit 2; repeat sequence across the row.

Repeat rows 1–8 twice or until desired length, ending with row 4 or row 8.

Bind off all stitches knitwise.

FINISHING

Weave short edges together.

Weave in loose ends.

With wrong side facing out, steam lightly.

- NATURAL FACEPACKS -

Fresh, all-natural ingredients such as fruits and herbs are perfect for homemade facepacks. Try the following:

STRAWBERRY MASK

Mash 4 to 6 strawberries and apply the pulp to your face (avoiding the eyes). Leave for 10 minutes and rinse off with water, or rosewater (see p.99), to leave your skin sparkling beautifully.

AVOCADO MASK

Scoop the flesh out of a ripe avocado and mash into a creamy pulp. Cover your face and leave for 15 to 20 minutes, then rinse with warm water and spritz with toner to close the pores.

HONEY SCRUB

Mix one tablespoon of honey with two tablespoons of finely ground almonds and half a teaspoon of lemon juice. Rub gently over face to exfoliate and then leave for 15 to 20 minutes before rinsing off with warm water.

- PRESSING FLOWERS -

Pick a selection of your favorite flowers and foliage and place them in the refrigerator to keep fresh until you are ready to make your press.

Arrange the flowers on one half of a sheet of newspaper, being careful that the leaves and petals do not overlap. Then fold the top half of the newspaper sheet down over the flowers.

Place the newspaper in the middle of a large, heavy book, such as a phone directory, then place a few other heavy books or objects on top for extra pressure.

After about three days, open the book and carefully remove your pressed flowers.

- SUGAR BODY SCRUB -

2½ CUPS (250 G) WHITE CANE SUGAR
2½ CUPS (250 G) AVOCADO OIL
2 TEASPOONS ALOE VERA GEL
2 DROPS LAVENDER ESSENTIAL OIL
2 DROPS ESSENTIAL OIL

Combine all of the ingredients in a bowl.

Scoop some of the scrub out using your hand and massage gently onto your skin for a minute (the scrub will actually tighten onto your skin like a mask).

Leave on for 3 to 4 minutes before rinsing. The scrub can be used all over your body, and is suitable for most skin types.

If you don't have the above ingredients, you can just add sugar to your cleanser for a moisturising exfoliating scrub for smooth skin.

NOTE: If you have sensitive skin, test the scrub on a small area first.

- HOMEMADE MOISTURIZER -

4 TEASPOONS WHEAT GERM OIL
4 TABLESPOONS AVOCADO OIL
$1\frac{1}{4}$ CUPS (25 G) COCOA BUTTER
1 TEASPOON BEESWAX
$\frac{1}{2}$ TEASPOON BORAX POWDER
2 TABLESPOONS ROSEWATER
10 DROPS GERANIUM ESSENTIAL OIL
5 DROPS FRANKINCENSE ESSENTIAL OIL
5 DROPS SANDALWOOD ESSENTIAL OIL

Combine the wheat germ and avocado oil in a heat resistant-bowl, and place in a saucepan that has been half-filled with water.

Place over a medium heat, and add the cocoa butter and beeswax until the mixture has blended.

Dissolve the borax in the rosewater and add to the mixture by stirring all ingredients together.

Remove the saucepan from the heat and add the essential oils.

Let cool before storing.

NOTE: Avocado is an ideal treatment for tired or dry skin as it contains many of the oils lost through everyday life.

- BRINGING COLOR INTO YOUR HOME -

When thinking up color schemes for your home, it's often best to keep substantial items, such as the carpet, sofa, and arguably curtains, neutral, and then add vibrancy via colored walls and accessories. This will keep expenses down if and when you decide to change your color scheme.

Accent walls can break up the color in a room. Test potential colors on the desired wall, then let samples dry completely and look at them in both natural and artificial light before making a decision.

Objects that you should consider when matching or introducing a color scheme are soft furnishings (cushions, throws, rugs, bedding); ornaments (prints, framed photos, lamps, clocks, vases, sculptures); kitchenware (kettle, toaster, storage jars, bread bin, fruit bowls, dish towels); tableware (tablecloths, place mats, crockery, salt and pepper shakers); and floral arrangements, with endless color options.

There are different approaches you can take when introducing a color scheme. You can use just one main color throughout, or different tones of the same color. Alternatively you can place extra splashes of "accent" color(s)—to complement the dominant color, or even equal amounts of two or more contrasting colors, making sure that there are no uneasy clashes.

When making your choices for each room, you may wish to consider the main emotional impact that specific colors are believed to have. For example:
- ✎ Red: fiery and invigorating
- ✎ Orange: warm and reassuring
- ✎ Green: nourishing and soothing
- ✎ Blue: calming and cooling
- ✎ Yellow: sunny and uplifting
- ✎ Brown: grounding and practical

- CLASSIC MARTINI -

ICE CUBES
1 TEASPOON DRY VERMOUTH
$\frac{1}{3}$ CUP (80 ML) GIN
A TWIST OF LEMON PEEL

Half-fill a mixing glass with ice, add the dry vermouth, stirring to coat the ice, then strain out the excess and discard.

Pour the gin over the vermouth-coated ice, stir, then strain into a chilled cocktail glass. Garnish with a twist of lemon.

NOTE: To make a "Dirty Martini" add a splash of olive brine, plus an olive for garnish; this gives the cocktail a cloudy, "dirty" appearance.

- SIMPLE SALAD DRESSING -

---

3 TABLESPOONS GOOD QUALITY OLIVE OIL
1 TABLESPOON CIDER VINEGAR
1 TEASPOON DIJON MUSTARD
SALT AND PEPPER TO TASTE

Simply add all the ingredients together and mix well. If not using immediately, keep in the refrigerator for up to a week, but be sure to bring it up to room temperature and shake well before drizzling on your salad.

- MAKING ROSEWATER -

FRESH ROSE PETALS, WASHED
WATER
ICE CUBES

Place a Pyrex loaf dish upside down (or something heavy of a similar size) in the center of a large pan as a pedestal, and place a heatproof glass bowl on top of it.

Add the rose petals into the pan, around the loaf dish, so that they reach almost the top of the pedestal, and add just enough water to cover them.

If the lid to your pan is rounded, place it on upside down so that it's inverted; otherwise, place a stainless steel bowl on top of the pan—large enough to seal it but shallow enough so that its bottom does not touch the other bowl.

Turn up the heat to bring the water to a boil.

Add the ice cubes into the inverted lid or the top bowl: As the rose-infused steam rising from the water hits the underside of the cold lid/bowl, it should condense and drop into the internal bowl.

Turn down to a simmer and leave for two to four hours. Every now and again, carefully lift the lid and take out a little rosewater, stopping when the rose scent of the liquid begins to weaken. Replace the ice and boiling water if needs be as you do this; do not let the water boil dry.

- TROPICAL MOJITO -

---

8 MINT LEAVES
HALF A LIME, CUT INTO WEDGES
1 TABLESPOON (15 ML) SUGAR SYRUP (A WELL-COMBINED
MIXTURE OF EQUAL PARTS WHITE SUGAR AND WATER),
OR GUARAPO (SUGAR CANE JUICE)
ICE CUBES
4 TABLESPOONS (60 ML) WHITE RUM
SODA WATER TO TASTE

Place the mint, lime, and sugar syrup (or guarapo for a more natural flavor) in a cocktail shaker.

Mash these ingredients together either using a muddler or the end of a rolling pin or pestle. This releases the flavors of the various components.

Add a scoop of ice and pour in the rum.

Shake vigorously and strain into a chilled glass until about an inch from the top. Top up with soda water.

Garnish with a lime wedge or a sprig of mint if desired.

NOTE: To make a "Dirty Mojito" use key limes, brown sugar syrup, and spiced rum with the crushed mint, ice cubes, and soda. Or to make a Virgin Moijto, or "Nojito," follow the recipe above but omit the rum.

- FIVE USES FOR A LEMON -

❧ To clean chrome: Make a paste of baking soda and lemon juice, rub it in, rinse, and dry.

❧ To give dishes extra sparkle: Slice off a bit of lemon rind and place it in the cutlery section of your dishwasher; remove after one wash.

❧ To keep food fresh: Sprinkle lemon juice over cut fruit and vegetables that might turn brown before serving, such as apples, pears, and avocados.

❧ To prevent rice from sticking: Add a few drops of lemon juice when boiling rice to stop it from sticking to the pot; clean-up will be a lot easier as a result.

❧ To remove the smell of garlic from hands: Soak your hands in lemon juice for a few minutes, then wash with warm, soapy water.

- CREATING FRESH SCENTS -

❧ A simple bunch of scented flowers: Try freesias, jasmine, lilies, roses, or scented geraniums.

❧ Pots of scented herbs: bergamot, lavender, lemon verbena, mint, rosemary, sage, thyme

❧ Incense sticks: Burning incense is not to everyone's taste but it's worth experimenting to find one you like.

❧ Scented candles: patricularly organic aromatherapy candles, from lavender and rose for relaxation, to grapefruit and mint for invigoration

❧ Lavender bags (see p. 14): Keep these in your drawers and airing cupboard for sweet-smelling clothes and bedding.

- MAKING A REAL FIRE -

AT LEAST 3 OR 4 SHEETS OF NON-GLOSSY NEWSPAPER
AT LEAST 8 SMALL PIECES OF DRY KINDLING WOOD
UP TO $^3/_4$ INCH (2 CM) THICK
LARGER PIECES OF DRY WOOD OR COAL

Loosely scrunch the newspaper into ball shapes and arrange in the bottom of the grate.

Build the kindling into a little "wigwam" around the newspaper or in criss-cross stacks on top of it, leaving gaps for air to pass through. Position some larger sticks, logs, and coal (if using) around this.

Open the flue by adjusting the lever or knob if there is one. This will increase the air flow to your fire, ensuring that no smoke pours back into your room.

Light the newspaper in several places (use a fire screen as kindling can spark very easily). Once the kindling begins to burn well, add successively larger pieces of sticks, wood, and coal, each time waiting until these are burning well before adding more.

Gradually close the air flow to a minimum as the flames begin to grow.

NOTE: Be sure to have your chimney swept regularly—at least once a year, or more if you burn wood often. That way you can rest assured that there are no blockages, such as bird's nests, before lighting it.

- CREATING A GREETING CARD -

GOOD QUALITY CARD
SCISSORS
GLUE
COLORED PENS
ATTRACTIVE ALPHABET STICKERS OR INTERESTING
LETTERS CUT FROM OLD NEWSPAPERS AND MAGAZINES
A FEW NICE OLD BUTTONS, SCRAPS OF FABRIC, AND
PIECES OF RIBBON

Cut a piece of card to the desired size, remembering that you will need to fold it in half for it to stand up. Fold it neatly.

First establish what message you want to convey on the front of your card, such as "Happy Birthday," "Good Luck," or something more personal such as "The Birthday Girl Loves Cake" or a message containing the recipient's name.

Then write the message in colored ink or spell out the message in cut-out letters or stickers. Always decide where you want each word to appear before starting so that you don't run out of space.

Next, decide which of your craft items will work best with your message. For example, you could cut out small triangles of quaint fabrics and stick them along a thin strand of ribbon to create a vintage bunting effect to mark a celebration. Or you could cluster several pretty buttons together to make little flower heads, then draw on the stems and leaves. Let your imagination run wild, taking inspiration from the recipient's personal preferences.

Once finished, sign and date the back of the card as well as writing your greeting inside.

- TAKING PLANT CUTTINGS -

The best time to take cuttings is from late June to early August, when plants
like hydrangeas, lavender, roses, fuchsia, and forsythia produce firm shoots that
will readily root in some potting soil.

Choose stems that have not yet flowered and make a straight cut 2–4 inches
(5–10 cm) from the top, just beneath a pair of leaves. Remove any leaves from the
bottom of the stems and just leave a few pairs right at the top.

Dip the bottom of the stems in hormone rooting powder or liquid, which encourages
new roots to form and can be purchased from all good garden stores.

Select a 3-inch (7.5-cm) pot with drainage holes and fill with a mixture of potting
soil and horticultural grit (this helps the plants to drain better). Plant a few cuttings
around the edge of each pot, making sure not to get any leaves beneath the surface
of the soil. The more cuttings you plant, the more chance you'll have of success!

Water generously, then sit the pot in a plastic bag and secure with a rubber band
at the top—this will ensure the soil stays moist.

Place on a sunny windowsill and wait....

Ensure the soil stays moist by watering regularly and keep checking for roots—
you should see these coming through the drainage holes in the bottom of the pot
after a few weeks, or you can test by gently pulling at the cuttings and measuring
their resistance.

Plant each rooted cutting into its own 3-inch (7.5-cm) pot and transplant into a larger
pot again (see p. 78) when the roots start growing through the drainage holes.

Once each plant has grown to at least 6 inches (15 cm) tall, pinch out the top tip
to encourage new branches to grow.

- SEWING ON A BUTTON -

Choose a thread to match the original and look at other buttons on the garment to establish the stitch pattern—usually parallel or cross-wise on a four-hole button. Mark the position for the button using a pin.

Insert 18–24 inches (45–60 cm) of thread through a needle, then double the thread and knot the ends together.

Make a couple of small stitches one on top of the other to secure the thread behind where the button will be.

Now insert the needle through one of the holes in the button, from back to front, until the button rests on the pin.

Holding the button in place, push the needle down through another button hole, this time from front to back, then through to the reverse of the garment.

Make a small stitch and return the needle up through the fabric and again the button.

Repeat this "down and up" motion several times until it is secure, with an equal number of threads through each hole.

Finish your last stitch between the fabric and button. Remove the pin.

Make a small stitch behind the button, then wind the thread tightly, several times, around the stem of stitches between the button and fabric (called the 'shank').

To finish, make several tight stitches right through the shank itself and cut off the unused thread.

- Using Bath Salts -

When you're tired and your muscles are aching, there's nothing quite like a long soak in a hot bath. The addition of homemade bath salts can make the experience all the more luxurious.

Simply mix a drop or two of your favorite essential oil(s) with a handful or two of Epsom Salts and add to your running bath water. The salts help to relax the muscles and eliminate toxins from the body, while the oils add a touch of heavenly aromatherapy.

If you want to upgrade from standard Epsom salts, deluxe options include: sparkling, high-quality Ultra Epsom Salt and Himalayan Salt—a lovely pale pink salt said to contain some 84 minerals needed by the body!

- Homemade Bubble Bath -

---

1 PART CASTILE SOAP, GRATED
1 PART DISTILLED OR FILTER WATER
SOME GLYCERIN AND/OR SWEET ALMOND OIL
SEVERAL DROPS OF YOUR CHOSEN ESSENTIAL OIL(S)

Dissolve the grated soap in the water; warm water will speed the process. Alternatively, use liquid castile soap. Then mix in the glycerin and/or oil. Ingredient quantities can be varied depending on the desired amount and consistency.

Add your desired essential oil(s). Lavender or rose are good for relaxation; peppermint or eucalyptus for stimulation. Ask in your local health store if you are unsure.

Store in a dark glass bottle for at least 24 hours before using.

To use, shake gently and pour a generous amount under hot running bath water.

- SPICED CIDER -

---

4 CUPS (1 LITER) CIDER
4 TABLESPOONS HONEY OR 3 TABLESPOONS BROWN SUGAR
THE PEEL OF 1 ORANGE
1 APPLE, THINLY SLICED
2-3 CINNAMON STICKS
A HANDFUL OF WHOLE CLOVES
2 TEASPOONS GROUND ALLSPICE
⅓ CUP (80 ML) BRANDY
EXTRA CINNAMON STICKS AND ORANGE SLICES, FOR DECORATION

Place all ingredients into a saucepan.

Heat gently for approximately 20 minutes, stirring occasionally and ensuring that all sugar, if used, is dissolved.

Do not boil as this would burn off the alcohol and may turn the spices slightly bitter.

When ready, strain into glasses or cups, garnish with extra cinnamon sticks or orange slices, and enjoy.

You can keep the pot warm for quite a few hours at a low heat. Then people can refill their glasses if and when they feel the urge throughout the evening.

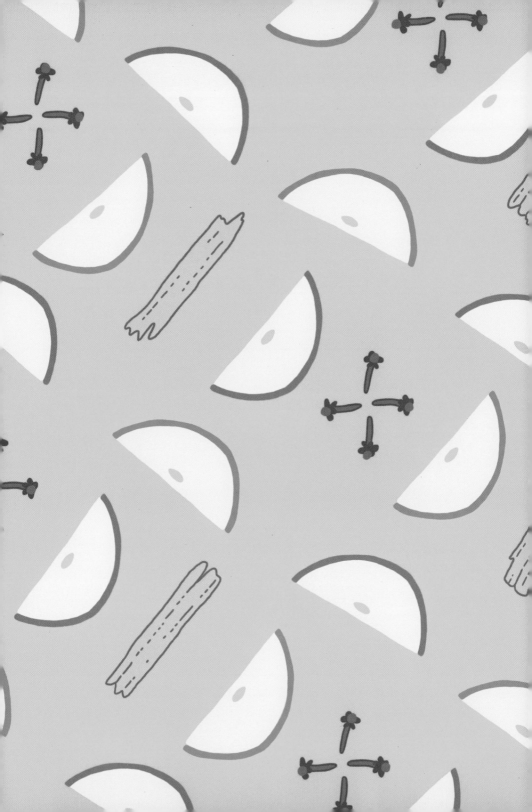

- ICING A CAKE -

$^2/_3$ CUP (140 G) BUTTER, SOFTENED
$2^1/_4$ CUP (280 G) CONFECTIONER'S SUGAR
1-2 TABLESPOONS MILK
A FEW DROPS VANILLA EXTRACT (OPTIONAL)
A FEW DROPS FOOD COLORING (OPTIONAL)

MAKING THE BUTTERCREAM

Beat the butter in a large bowl until soft. Mix in half the confectioner's sugar.

Add the remaining confectioner's sugar and the milk, and beat until smooth.

If desired, add a few drops of vanilla extract and/or food coloring,
mixing until well combined.

APPLYING THE BUTTERCREAM

Use a spatula to apply a thin layer of the buttercream to your freshly cooled
cake. This "crumb layer" seals in any crumbs.

Chill the cake until the crumb layer sets.

Finally, apply a thicker layer of buttercream, using the spatula or a palette knife
to gain as smooth a finish as possible.

- Making soap -

One method of making soap, called melt and pour, allows you to melt down a soap base and add your own choice of fragrance, shape, and color, without having to make it from scratch. All you need is the soap base and the molds, as well as whatever embellishments you wish to add, such as fragrance oils and colors.

Depending on how many bars you want to make, and the size of your molds, cut off an appropriate amount of soap base and divide it into small chunks. Put these in a microwaveable bowl and place in the microwave. Do not overheat it—the base just needs to melt, so heat it for a few seconds at a time.

Once the soap base is fully melted, you can add any fragrance or color that you wish, as well as any other additions such as dried flower petals. You can use simple food colors or liquid soap colors, and essential oils for fragrance. As a rough guide, use around 2 teaspoons of fragrance per pound of soap (20 ml per kilo).

Stir in your additions quickly before a skin forms, and then pour into the mold(s) you are using and allow to cool. You can place the molds in the refrigerator to speed this up (although once your soap is finished it should be kept at room temperature, so do not store it in the refrigerator).

Once it is cool, remove the soap from the mold.

- INDEX -